hiding out
selected poetry

Bunny Pearlman

ISBN: 979-8-9933477-1-4

The cover and title page font is Century Gothic;
poem titles are set in New Times Roman;
poems are in Helvetica Neue.

Sharpgiving Press

Hiding Out: selected poetry

Foreword

Reading Bunny Pearlman's *Hiding Out: selected poetry* is a lot like taking a long walk with the poet. A walk over four decades and through various locales. Some recognizable and familiar, ordinary and plain, others exotic, compelling and strange. It is her intelligence and seriousness that raises the poems above a travelogue or journal, we get to see her absorb what she experiences as love, as nature, as the passage of time, without adornment and self-explanation. As is so often true her honesty doesn't bring happiness. Half the time she uses the poem as a microscope examining, and half the time it's a telescope. Love and tumult put to the side, family seems to survive best. In one poem she seems most at peace at the end of the day sitting on the stoop with her older brother arguing science. And at the end of the book she writes "Will I live long enough/to re-negotiate the secrets/of childhood." It is a question only someone who has stayed mindful, and is still brave, can pose.

Keith Althaus

Introduction

My father wrote humorous poetry—influenced by the great American humorist and punster Ogden Nash, ("Who wants my jellyfish? I'm not sellyfish!") He (my dad) regularly produced two-liners and even a few minor epics—for family events, letters to us in school and camp and for his colleagues at work. Somewhere there is a folder of his writings. I think my sister Nancy had it. I'm not sure where it is now. But I remember a couple of lines of a poem he sent to me when I was eighteen and directing a summer camp production of *The King and I.*

> The wabbit with the golden hair
> hops awound like Fred Astaire
> The king and I and me togetera
> etcetera etcetera etcetera

From there to the fact that my brother Harry, my sister, Edie, and I wrote poetry from the time we were children and won prizes in school and belonged to poetry societies later in high school and college.

It is perhaps not so big a leap as it might seem. We loved to play with language. Early on in the form of elaborate puns shared at the dinner table and whenever the smallest opening, a propitious moment we could sneak in a good groaner. We played with language—playmates and friends that became lovers of language and writers even on to the next generations including my grandchildren who write poetry effortlessly and share easily.

Much of my writing remains in journals and unpublished letters to family, friends and lovers. But two collections—the early poems of the seventies and eighties from The Russian River and Provincetown and The Montclair Poems that include some from Mexico and California were preserved in neat manuscripts and labeled manilla envelopes.

For a good part of these neatly assembled and preserved collections I owe Gordon Carrega, poet, whom I married in 1973 in Monte Rio in the Russian River area of California. He introduced me to the life of the poet as opposed to someone who writes poetry. We participated together in poetry readings around the bay area, Sonoma County and the Russian River and published a page in *The Russian River Stump* that I illustrated featuring friends of Gordon's, Hunce Voelcker, and Andrei Codrescu. We also contributed to a lively small magazine from the Russian River called *Paper Pudding*. But mostly Gordon enabled me to step out of the box labeled visual artist and dancer/choreographer and allowed me to take myself seriously as a writer of poetry. The poems written in Montclair were shared weekly with Gordon after we had found each other again —following a twenty year silence. For a brief time we continued to share work on a regular basis via email.

A small collection of poems from Israel survived neatly typed (with a few translated into Hebrew by WUJS (World Union of Jewish Students) director Rav Aubrey Isaacs. Thanks to the staff of WUJS in Arad and to London performance poet Leah Thorn who managed to make them take us seriously. The last section of the manuscript represents my recent work (Mexico, Berkeley, New Jersey, Provincetown.) And I continue to cull my surviving journals and notebooks for gems or could be gems—The latest inclusion in the manuscript from the Galilee ancient city of Safed—is *Hospital Tzfat*. Finally, the fact that I am putting it all together in one cohesive manuscript is owed in no small part to Truro (Cape Cod) poet Keith Althus who twice annually offers a free workshop for senior poets at Castle Hill in Truro, its members chosen by some mysterious lottery. In which all the trappings etc. come together to form an almost religious atmosphere punctuated by humor and pathos.

But—I write poetry because I love writing poetry. The process tickles a part of my brain that is untouched by the painter, dance maker part. Its process is closer to the sudoku and wordle solving part than it is to my prose writing brain—it is deductive and intuitive and playful even when the poems are intense and self-exposing. A line of poetry is right when it feels right and sounds right. Its musicality and its provocative allusions may be worked at or upon but the real meat of poetry is about the puzzle, the way it all fits together with as little pomp —so that it comes across as beshert—meant to be— discovered rather than manufactured or manipulated. All the parts of the puzzle fit together in the only possible way. When the life of a painting feels this way I often refer to it as its poetry.

Bunny Pearlman

The cover
The cover is designed by Shiala Grey-Sky King, Lakota Sioux painter and designer. The painting is "Cubist House" by Bunny Pearlman.

Hiding Out I

(in the beginning)

Allowing the world only glimpses,
The perfect courtesan
I will not allow you to be bored.

You politely curtail
my continuous monologue,
I offer my body,

Now you are in love with me again.

I remember to sweep beneath the stove.
I must amaze you in small ways.

Monte Rio (Russian River), CA, 1974
published in Grandmother Spider, *White Bear*
Books, 1976

Hiding Out II

Today the sun denies us
and there is no wood for the fire

The cat leaps to my back
over my shoulder
follows my brush
I have surrounded you with purple
in your absence
Japanese colors are cheap
but fugitive
fading a little more
each hour of each day

Now I add blue as you sleep
and tighten the rocks behind your head

The water begins to move
breaking against the gray sand
Two thumb tacks to the wall
in line with your waking vision

(Brackenwood, Monte Rio, CA)
Russian River
New Collage, Sarasota, FL, 1974

Hiding Out III
The Perfect Hermits

Now I cling to you
My body is leaner
I feel you feel
my new bones

Your skin as always
but rediscovered
The smooth covering
so civilized

Just my paintings
and your poems
the perfect Hermits

Cazadero, CA, 1974; Monte Rio, Russian River, CA
New Collage, Sarasota, FL, 1976

3

Crumbling Convent Walls

Crumbling convent walls
slivered with glass
where birds sipped the blood
from my hands

strapped in thorazine
I put on my velvet jacket
and pace the stained
glass corridors

you are banished
jailer, fixed with the
stubborn insistence of my
emptied eyes

I fly towards the sun
lion astride
gilded in the shimmering
mane of his reluctance

play slowly
in the garden of selectivity

Grandmother Spider, *Monte Rio, CA, 1971*
Paper Pudding, *Monte Rio (Russian River), CA, 1973*
reprinted by Nevermind, *Sacramento, CA, 1974*

Tepic to Tijuana

Endless humid journey
ballooning feet, numbed coccyx
visions retina racing freely past—tensing
North—Tepic to Tijuana

Mexican rock stars
foot tapping
sotto rehearsing in the dark

a blue and green parakeet
in a small cage next to
Cantinflas reading
sado-masochistic comic books

Tired journey soiled parents
adoring father
standing all the way to Mexicali

midnight paranoia
Federales searching our luggage
a tangle of red hair in this sea of dark—and

we speak no spanish
Guilty !

San Blas, Mexico, 1974

Remember *(for Edie)*
Memento Mori

Remember
Georgie Porgie
and walking to school
you held my hand across the dry lot

Remember I was afraid
thinking the threat of his kiss
a real one

Remember
Blue you're a jew
and dad's C.D. helmet
it was white

Remember
the clover lawns
and the bee stings
on the bottoms of our feet

My first party dress
made from my mother's curtains (shades of Tara)

and Carol Tapley next door
who destroyed—my best doll
at my birthday party

I sat and played quietly
while you hung from the trees
by your scarred knees
I danced to the radio

(Hempstread, Long Island, NY)
Provincetown First Winter, 1976

The Desert—The Color of Memory (Arad)

Though today it rests quietly
while the waiting wind
gathers itself

Look closer
to the smallest particles of rock
in a meeting of particles
gravely intimate
calling itself sand
when it can remember its origin
and love its ubiquity

See how its color joins with nature
by adding the color of sand
saturating the landscape
extinguishing passion
nulling personality

The color of memory
faded by time like old photos
and letters and pajamas
softened by utility and age
and loss

Still it catches in your throat
when you try to sing
should your heart fill
with a moment of remembering

it has escaped
a thousand
lifetimes of inequity

Arad (The Negev), Israel, 1998

Above My Table (for Zeev)
Memento Mori

1
Above my table
where I write each morning
is a painting of my studio
in the desert

There is an empty room
and two black ladder—back chairs
One is next to the fireplace
where I built a fire
each winter morning
of lemon wood
floated from Turkey

Where I sat with my coffee
huddled in an army blanket
coaxing my stiffened fingers
and my reluctant brain

Through the huge arched window
is the desert and the caves
and about midway to the horizon
an oasis with tall cedars and palms

A spot of green nestled
in a small depression
the Arad cemetery
surrounded by treeless hills
and ancient mounds of sand and rock

Where I sit on Shabbat
watching the birds
who forgive my intrusion

2
I have a friend buried here
An old Russian, Zeev
who built my workbench

at first Oxana from across the way
comes to interpret

but soon she is bored
and we are left alone

We communicate haltingly
with a melange of gestures
bits and pieces of three languages
and a strange urgency
amused by our dilemma
although perhaps only laughing
out of pleasure

He was a nuclear engineer
in the old country
now he tinkers every day
with beaten up old cars
persuading them to run again

The day of his funeral
I sat protected against the howling wind
and the driving rain sitting by the fire
talking to my sister on Cape Cod
describing the scene
through the great arched windows of my studio
the winding road—bumper to bumper
The Russian community streaming to his graveside

My new friend and I
were just getting to know each other
We were so carefully getting to know each other
fostering a precious thing
a sweet kernel at the center of a new place
A new world
When his heart gave out

3
An empty room with two chairs
There are three strong shadows
on the pink tile floor
that I have painted in a purple gray
Behind the chair by the fireplace
beside the chair in the foreground
and the shadow of an unseen ladder
with five rungs widely spaced
crosses the floor

Arad, Israel, 2001 (down the street from Amos Oz);
Provincetown, MA, 2002

9

Poppies

House sitting in Berkeley
feeding Jack's turtle
and watering the garden
when it doesn't rain
Last night while I slept
in my nephew's bed
under the down comforter
covered in orange flannel

the red poppies opened
in the back garden
They are a foot taller than
the orange California poppies
with the pale feathery leaves

Today it rained
flattening their exuberance
diminishing their brilliance
I must wait
for the next bent and fuzzy head
to reach to the sun
and fill to bursting

I see them in my sleep
waiting for me
There is a mystery there
of the past growing into the future
the empty rooms
at my brother's house
the unhappy garden

Or the small babe
who will soon return to the empty crib
in the next room
I want to curl into it to warm it for her
Imagine counting your time on earth
in days and weeks

Do you sometimes remember
that heart breaking innocence
a flash of a hummingbird
who has mistaken your hat
for another bit of garden

It's all his garden you know
we are keeping it bright for him
and waiting

In the late afternoon
I dozed over my book
a story about Africa
I hear him first
buzzing and clicking around my head

I am grateful the way a child is
awed by its first butterfly
landing on the window sill
and the way the light
breaks into spirit particles
through the blinds

She will stare for hours in her crib
breaking into a chain of
small laughter
like the clover chain
she will some day
tie together in her garden

Her smooth face flushed red
by the heat
and the poppies reflection
A laugh that grows stronger
with each delight
And we will join her
Remembering

Berkeley, CA, 2000

11

The First Shabbat (Elder Camp CT)
(meditation I)

I wake slowly
adjusting to geese
and bullfrogs

This morning a canoe
drifts through the morning haze
slicing the lake surface
rippling the polished reflection
of the trees

A father in an indigo blue shirt
with his small son between his knees
in an orange life jacket
move soundlessly across the lake

The Second Shabbat
(meditation II)

I went back to sleep
and slept through the bird's morning assembly
the barking crow, I think, is never satisfied

unlike the tiny checkered bird
who skims across the lake
Its smile reflected
in the glassy surface

the ripple that it creates
stretches exponentially to the shore
where the deer I saw
when I was swimming
lifts his head
and stares in my direction
before turning sharply into the wood

Lightning and Rainbows
(meditation III)

Yesterday afternoon a bolt of lightning
on its way to the center of the earth
collided with an ancient spruce tree
and split it down its center
as I watched through
my cabin window

Last evening while we chanted
a rainbow filled the sky
outside the glass walled synagogue
There is no way to explain this miracle
of synchronicity

Later the splintered moon rising
on the lake outside my window
a million celebratory fireflies
and a beaver tucking its head into the water

the breeze blowing across the lake
separating patterns of blue and green

the geese stand and watch

Camp Isabella Freedman
Falls Village, CT, 2006

A Smiling Moon (the beginning)
Momento Mori

1
Every action leads to a reaction
my father explained it to me
he was an engineer
and a believer in physics

Interrupt one small ripple in the creek
and somewhere on the other shore
a newly hatched turtle
still soft and yielding
enters the water without stopping

a water bug has two more inches
to skimmer across
and the world is changed forever

2
In the corner of the hall closet
behind the dank smelling coats
behind the moldy parkas
and the camel's hair
smelling of camphor

I experimented
with sitting totally motionless
breathing soundlessly
even sometimes holding my breath
to stop the world
like the Don Juan
of Castaneda

If I did not move
if I sat perfectly still
perhaps the world would stop moving
and I could prevent
a catastrophe

if we all held our breath
every one of us
on the same day
at precisely the same hour

and minute and second
the world might stop

And barring, an earthquake, a typhoon
the earth shifting too suddenly on its axis
we could report a minute or two
in modern history when nothing happened
and no reaction was left behind
no detritus
debris
artifact
Nothing to prove our world
ever existed

Still science might argue
that simply occupying space
exchanging molecules of heat
breathing through our skin
there is no way to stop the world
and leave nothing behind
a breath
a purr
a longing
a sadness

My brother the born existentialist
and I would argue the point
into the summer's night
on the stoop
beneath a smiling moon

Berkeley, CA, 2005

Memorial Day

Flying over the town
chasing my reflection on the glassy water
I slam into it like a loon
hitting the surface hard
with a desperate wind shattering (wings flapping)
moment—before landing

I am drinking coffee with Junior
that is he stares at me
with his round amber cat eyes
waiting to jump into my lap
at the precise moment
I lift the cup to my lip

All morning he has been barking
mouth fluttering
at the one bird who comes every day
to torment him

I watch my little family still sleeping
Lise cocooned in a star quilt
she carried with her from South Dakota
The shape of her long body beneath it
purple and white

Shiala wrapped in the fuzzy red blanket
from Jordan purchased at the glatt market
in Tzfat one freezing fall evening

And Nathan all but obliterated
by his yellow Spongebob backpack
that never leaves his side

Only his small feet
peeking out from under the coverlet
give him away
retreating from babyhood
losing their squarish baby shape

Provincetown, 2003

16

Pale Nimbus (Creation)
(meditation IV) (nocturnal vision)

Pale Nimbus
before speech
before the tongue pierced
the wall of silence
creating longing and pathos
and enigma

a door opening
or maybe only a passing car
awakens a sleeping phantom
a paper ghost descending
with each step a reminder
of the one before
to the basement
where the striations of the generations
bleed through the spongy walls

I sit quietly in the darkest corner
bathed in a narrow ray of light
from a small window
near the ceiling
green like the green of french velvet

or maybe softer like the carpet of moss
beneath the redwoods
where we walked hand in hand
Hansel and Gretel

your hand feels small in mine
yet I know it to be larger and square
with blunt fingers
and pale nails with moons
but that is some time later

I sit with my back to the damp wall
peering into the coal dark
but I see nothing—until the dance begins
one small brave spark
from a million miles away
and a millennium
spawn of the nimbus

17

awakened by my intrusion
renegade, escapee
without benefit of partner
splits into two—It is the beginning
breisheet

Now each small spark has found a mate
and so forth—and so on
reproducing with unrestrained naked abandon
They are everywhere
bowing to each other and calling in squeaky voices
I hear them before I see them
And then I see them before
my tears blind me

Berkeley, CA, 2006

It Is Getting Late in the Day
Memento Mori

It is getting late in the day
the sun has retreated to the other side
of the earth

The frozen days are lengthening
and the icicles are disappearing
into little pools
at the bottom of the spruce

I have a lingering story to tell you
It's about an old man
who used to follow us around
in the summers
by the lake
Ronkonkoma

He let us tie him to a tree
one Fourth of July weekend
after the war
when our parents
had forgotten about us

They remembered just in time
to stop us from successfully
lighting the match
Very little was ever said about it

We were a gang that summer
presided over by my older sister
Perhaps that is why she cringes
when I tell the story

coda:
now that my sister is gone
and my brother—who was maybe seven then
there is no one else left to remember
how we almost crossed the line
into the inconceivable

Montclair, NJ, 2005 (coda—2015, Union City)

19

The Rooms of My Childhood

Of the first room
I remember only a crib
below an open window
with a moving cloud of a curtain
blown by a summer breeze

But it may have been my brother's crib
or my baby sister's
Each of us on the heels
of the other
with barely enough time
to anticipate
to adjust

And through the window
my mother hanging the laundry
turning her head quickly
to avoid the wind driven wash
shoeless even in the snow

The way my father loved her best
barefoot and pregnant
My grandmother used to say

Of my second room
after we moved from the country
to the suburbs
I remember very little at first
sleeping while awake
leading orchestras
in a locked room

After being chased by a monitor
With an arm band
At recess—at the new school PS 170
and sliding in the gravel on my face
A lost period of time
a lost room

Of the room of my growing up
shared with my sisters
First one
Then both
I remember every tiny detail

I can count every knot
on the knotty pine walls
feel the fever in my wrists
as the knots whirl off into space

Of a black and tan puppy
its shuddering fur
woven through my hot fingers
a cooling glass of juice
the color of crayon
slipping down my fevered throat
the silly puppy
lapping it off my chin
wounding me with sharp claws
and puppy teeth

My oldest sister is as always
across the chasm
of the stairwell reading
The flashlight a telling glow
through the sheets

And my baby sister
who joined us later
in her narrow bed
beside the sloping wall
another chasm
of just five years
a stranger

We left her in that big room
and moved to our
rooms in the basement
built by my father
during the embarrassing years
of his unemployment

With our own entrance
and an exit on the back alley
transition to the grown up world
to come

Montclair, NJ, 2005

A Great Mansion (Memento Mori)
Alan Lichtenstein (a short but generous life)

Last night I dreamt again
of a great mansion
pink stone stained and
diminished by acid rain
ennobled by time

attended by crumbling
cherubs and warriors
great gilded lions at the gates
and a stone infant
lying beneath the broken udders
of a she wolf

I walked with a young friend
a former student
who leaned conspiratorially against me
as we continued down the path
that lead from our gatekeeper's house
to the glorious pink mansion
shrouded in the morning mist

Later I said
we will come back here later
Now we must visit a teacher
who is dying
he is nearby
and waiting for us

(the Ringling Museum)
1968 Alan Lichtenstein
New College, Sarasota, FL
(Montclair, NJ, 2005)

Isabelle (Hebrew School, Belleville, New Jersey)

How quick and bright
she is
A whirlwind
A sprite
A coiled spring
unwinding and rewinding
and swirling
like a nebula

Ooh ooh ooh
Her hand in the air
straining from her shoulder
a dark hollow
The pit of her child arm
long muscles and sinews
a DaVinci bird
Please! please let me
let me tell the story
She begs

It is the first warm day
The kids have shed winter
with alarming speed
I can see each blue vein
beneath her pale skin
the brave covering of her
child body

Tu Bishvat
Even if the Messiah is on his way
we must finish planting the tree (I quote
From the talmud)

Was Christ the Messiah —she asks

We have just finished Easter
The resurrection has made the headlines
before Moses and The Sea of Reeds

I buy discounted Easter candy for them
pastel green and blue and pink M&Ms
They like the bunnies on the back

23

I am politic and patient
in deference to pluralism
and mixed parentage
I hide in the context
in historical imperative

"I could be the Messiah"
Isabelle jumps up to tell us

Montclair, NJ, 2005

Jose (Angel in the Basement)

It is six-thirty in the morning
I am awakened by
the dark muffled figure
scraping the newly fallen snow
it is Jose who lives in the basement

I peek through the slats in the blinds
without turning on the light
the sky is black and empty
But the snow on the ground is dazzling
The bundled figure
scraping the sidewalk
casts no shadow

Jose, who is very handsome
never speaks to me
Or when he must
he looks away mumbling to
an invisible companion

One day I caught him in a smile
revealing the fact
that he is without teeth

I am told he has a girlfriend
But I have never seen him with anyone
Even hanging with the guys
he stands apart

I like to think he is a loner
that we understand each other
I like knowing he is down there
next to the furnace

Montclair, NJ, 2000

Bedtime

I have turned out the light
and punched up the pillow
and stretched my toes
to the end of the bed looking for sleep

In the darkened room
the stripes of light through the blinds
tell me my Indian neighbors
are still awake

The Nani is washing up in the kitchen
The sink is under the window
where she can look out
at her grandchildren in the afternoon
at the sky at night

She eschews the yellow gloves
her daughter in law hangs by the sink
preferring the caress
of the hot soapy water
on her swollen knuckles

She dries the dishes slowly
studying the remembered pattern
stacking them on the counter
forgetting where she is
then remembering

(The light goes out)

she holds her breath for a moment
and then sighing loudly
enough to alert her little white dog
who waits on the landing
He lifts his curly head and thumps his tail
against the stair

She clings tiredly to the handrail
lingering over its silken surface
worn smooth by the generations
upstairs her grandchildren are asleep
in separate rooms

She sings a song from childhood
softly to herself

26

punctuated by whimpers
from the waiting dog
and wonders where her life went
She is so far from the two rooms
where she was born

I see her smooth face in the morning
leading her grandchildren
to the big yellow bus
nodding to the Indian driver
And in the afternoon
as she awaits their return

During the day
when they are all away
And she has turned off the vacuum cleaner
her face changes in the empty house
encompassed by the music of her girlhood

Once I saw her through the window
dancing I lingered there enchanted
while she moved across the room
in an easy languid pattern stepping
and turning until I thought she saw me
watching

Now it is only the lonesome moon
behind the blinds
guarding the night almost complete
Still lacking a little bit
at the top

I pray for spring
The sun following me home
like a lover
warming my back

Montclair, NJ, 2006

27

A Secret Life
(meditation V)

A secret life
can be of the spirit
of the mind
of the heart

Or a Thursday
tango lesson in The Barrio
A dark haired stranger
who sits beside you
everyday on the bus
Though you never exchange
a word and only the edges
of your coats
touch each other

Or a small spot
high in the spruce tree
hung with icicles
and later
berries

I can put myself up there
with the birds
on a sunny day
hang out on a limb
and watch the sky move

I can see the cars below
softened into sleeping bears
the bird tracks in the snow
quickly filling in
My face tingles from new snow
blowing from the east
The world is mercifully
white again

Montclair, NJ, 2005

Has Someone Died (Memento Mori)

Last night I dreamt again
of my brother
He showed me the beauty
of the place we had left
The water sparkled
in the sunlight
The ground sloped
precariously in front of us
But he stood comfortably at the edge
like an athlete or a dancer
And then let go

On the left I watched for him to come up
On the right he still stood smiling at me
brilliantly happy
glorying in the beauty
of the place

Have you forgotten
how much you loved it here
He inquires
How magnificent the sunlight
reflects on the water
The grass grows almost to the edge
The water is rimmed
by a dark outline of mud

Our cottage is only a shack—
The floor rough and slanted
The walls covered with tatterred
posters and faded photos
When the tide is high
You can hear
The escaping water trickling
Under the wooden floor boards

We are gathered here
for a family occasion
We have cooked our best dishes
and wear our show off duds
there is plenty of wine
Has someone died

Provincetown, MA; Berkeley, CA

False and Illuminating Chimera (after the storm)

The weather was quiet and calm
when I left picking my way to the market

Bread and cheese and milk for my coffee
to last another day
swing in a plastic bag hanging from my wrist
my hands clenched deeply in my pockets

I am cautious
I pick up and put down my booted feet
leaving frankenstein shapes
in the compliant snow
and pause drinking in
the quietude

It is the second day after
a memory of blinds rattling
against the windows
in spite of double panes and storm sashes
Of cats curled tightly against my hips
through the long wintry night

I have pulled my heaviest socks over my trousers
ringed with insulating snow and ice
breaking as I walk into little balls — like popcorn
a remembered technique from childhood
uninvited bits of snow have crept
into my shoes

Then — without warning I am blind sighted
by a blast of frozen air
I bind my numbing face —
a lesson I learned in the desert
during a sandstorm
Pulling my muffler tight and knotting it

I try not to breathe
until it passes — and I can feel the sun again
making my cautious way across the street
blinking away the little bits of cruel ice
that attach themselves to my fattened lashes
avoiding the black icy spots

31

where the snow has departed in little gusts
by the exhaled breath of the tiny snow ogres
who followed us when we were children
on Long Island

Last week I slipped and fell on the ice
ass over tea kettle
and froze to the sidewalk
waiting for the ambulance
they covered me with delicious heated blankets
in the hospital—while my teeth chattered
like castanets

The world is soundless and benign
once again as I walk towards home
eye on the beacon my red door
pink now through the haze of white

Ah I have arrived at the walkway
cleared by the dark huddled figure of Jose
before the sun came up
and mounded dutifully on both sides
On my right
lies a small bit of yellow
in the shape of a wing—a butterfly wing
I stand staring at it
my muffler hardening against my mouth

What are the odds that it would survive
and land here carried on the wind
scrolled across it in black a secret code
acrostic heraldic cabalistic
I cry catching an icy breath
wanting to give it refuge wanting to touch it
I bow to the infinite
yud hay vav hay

it will be gone in a breath of yellow dust
I reach out, I cannot help it
mittens frozen into boxing gloves
numb and useless hands inside
a yellow gum wrapper glinting in the snow
a moment ago was the summer wing of a butterfly

Montclair, NJ, 2005

32

Making the Bed
(Memento Mori)

1

I make the bed every day
usually after coffee
always before lunch
Every day for most of my grown up life

Making the bed is easy
I sleep alone
No one to wrestle with
No waking in the night
to find they have cocooned themselves
in all three blankets
The fourth on the floor
with a cat or two snuggled down

If I get overheated in the night
I roll the covers down
and pull up my gown
breathing deeply
with my heart thumping
and my eyes stinging
I wait for it to pass
talking to myself
about life
about my life

Sometimes reassured
I fall into a deep sleep
and wake up naked to the neck
and shivering
Then I roll the covers back

2

in the morning—
no ruffled counterpane
no evidence of disturbance
The cats have pinned me down again
one on either side
I hear the birds chattering away
eating the berries
outside my window

And I know the sleeping cats
will soon be at them
Separated by a single pane of glass
They could crash through
Like superman—supercat
How I ran ecstatic into the blur
to taste them on my extended tongue
In later years
how I ran through the streets
pursued by a lover
Christopher Reeves died today

3

Incrementally colder
the days are shorter
I dreamt of a snowfall
that quickly covered a trailer, an Airstream
You could see its softly rounded shape
and a bit of smoke from the top
until that too disappeared

I try to remember
the beauty of winter
How the first snowflakes thrilled me
caught in a doorway
exchanging hot kisses
with the first snow
considered propitious

My landlord won't turn on the heat
until November
I can already feel the chill at my back
The draft on my neck as I type
I am wearing my sheepskin slippers
I can feel the bite at my ankles

My body isn't as warm as it once was
I must find a house sweater
In the bottom of the trunk
tonight I must add another blanket

Montclair, NJ, 2000

Begin Again
(meditation VI)

1

summer has gone
still she lies golden in the sand
catching the last rays
happy sister to the sun
while I truckle away shrinking into shadow

across the horizons
of my fevered dreaming
cavorting dolphins—grinning
as they do
framed in sea spray and pink in early light
join the dance

I crawl like a wad of old pinky black sidewalk gum
out from where I have been hiding
flattened against the insides of the horns
of a beaten up old conch shell
warmed by the sun and cooled by the sea
and look around
peering through the predawn mist
an army of ghosts float
across the lake

slow the mind down
match words to vision
arrange them in sync
with the rhythm
of the heart
I fold my hands to silence them
the bone ends of my fingers excuses
whisper something forgiving
and begin the dance

no wild corybantic tarantella
no lean abiding tango
no anarchic clatter
nothing sentimental
just the swaying of the pines to
the call and answer of the wind

2

flat-footed jays like ballet dancers
in the wings
chase my tufted titmice
who circle around them
and bounce smartly up to the feeder

leaves leave a planet of
shadows and patterns
on other leaves
where ants romance and cavort

just for the briefest of moments
a breath and a sigh really
I join them
not a bad life this

a heron flies through
the steadily lifting mist
leaving the memory of its shape
against the slate colored lake

The day goes on without trying
and night begins with the moon
I fall asleep to the hooting of owls

Nathan leaves for school
but first
I hear the clink of his spoon
against the sides of
the blue bowl
his huge feet bounding across the deck
and crunching gravel to the road

I carry my coffee
to my table facing the lake
arrange my brushes in descending order
next to the jar of clean water
the small palette on the right
and the larger on the left at my elbow and begin

Great Pond, Eastham, MA, 2014

The Park—*Old Men, Trees, Stones and Birds*
Memento Mori

1
Old trees like old men
deeply creviced and gnarled
brown like sparrows
the surviving color
I am haunted by Neruda
by the act of poetry
Every stone—is the first stone
the first pebble gathered on the beach

The suitcase of stones you carried
halfway across a continent
but you could not take it with you
the life you found
only a taste a
lingering on the tongue

2
I am never alone in the park
even in the early morning
with my tea
I bring my history
the trees eat my sorrow
the way my old cat
bites my fingers
gazes at me with her cataract eyes
and releases me

The old man almost opposite
sometimes sleeps sitting up
and shakes himself awake

He works in the park
carries his brown bag lunch
to this corner every day
to close his eyes and dream

The brown sparrows
who can survive anything and do

a war a holocaust
the crazy weather we have inherited

37

and make worse
the birds surround him as he nods off
the sandwich in his hand
they nibble at the crumbs
as they fall

The impecunious crow
rags on everyone
eats anything
dives at the old man
as he sleeps
they know each other
from before
same bench
same sandwich
in a lost time
they were friends

Now the rough mean sound
wakes him
he shields his eyes
a strong breeze fragrant
with jasmine and pine
caresses

July 12, 2015 (Neruda's Birthday) Union City, NJ

The Quiet Rhythm of All This

when I was a small child
ecstasy was an easy thing

I'd kick off my sandals
the leather fraying
like fringes
the open buckles
clacking against the slate walk

run through the wet grass
to the waiting swings
and release them
from their bondage
wound around the rusty green pole
and tied
til summer

so they would not be caught by the wind
and go madly and wildly back and forth
without me
until the ropes tired and frayed
unraveled near the top

and the wooden swings
with the knotted rope left in the holes
flew wildly into the March wind
and zigzagged through the used up fruit trees

to the farmer's field
the one where we stole carrots
at the end of summer
and ate them where we kneeled
tasting earth and abandon

the songs on the radio whispered to me
echoing my random thoughts
that brought movement to my feet
sliding across the linoleum

did we have a red ceiling in the kitchen
or was that later
My mother and I touching shoulders
at the sink
she handed me the slippery plates

I wiped and stacked them on the red counter
edged with something silver
chrome maybe

she was trying to tell me something
something important
her eyes were wet steel
her beauty laid bare
but I only saw the red counter
and the red ceiling

and her hands that were always red
the cuticles raw and splitting
though she ministered
to them nightly
with unguents from
mysterious cobalt jars
that looked Egyptian
while my father invented arias
in the shower

I thought him a great singer
and wondered why he wasn't
part of the moribund panorama
unfolding below
the night he took me to
the Met
I wore my first nylons

Then some months later
Carnegie hall
I sang in the choir
he brought me a yellow rose

they were becoming real to me
my father sitting in the balcony
my mother home
with the other kids
it would feel strange
when we returned

Union City, NJ, 2015

40

Hospital Tzfat (Safed) (Israel)

I have returned to the ward
with my coffee
My ward mates are whispering
looking up at me with narrowed eyes

I am chastised by the nurse
with the cupcake hat
for missing rounds
no one told me about rounds
that I was supposed to be there

Two Bulgarian woman
go in and out of the room
four or five times a day
I find it hard to tell them apart
They are shaped like boxes
This one dons a straw hat
with a flower on it

I look forward to these moments
how gracefully she winds the rag
around the squeegee
how easily it traverses the tile
it is a dance—fantasia
the floor show

My roommate
has returned from surgery
her mother and sister sit
at the end of my bed
whispering and waiting

my roommate groans and mutters
in her sleep
the end of my bed rocks
with their impatience

I have had an argument with a nurse
and I have been banished
to the Arab section
(they promise to bring me real coffee
in the morning)

There are ten beds in the new ward
families bring offerings
three times a day
and peel oranges between
and sleep next to the beds at night
and in the aisles

They are the lumpy shadows
I trip over on the way
to the bathroom

I am a curiosity here
I shall get fat on pastries
dripping with honey—washed down
with muddy coffee that bites the
back of your throat

Ah finally
My exile is over
I am back in my old room
moved closer to the nurses desk
This means they have scheduled
my surgery

Tzfat, Israel, 2001

Thoughts while painting—Definitions, Evolution

Perception
choices
unheard voices
things that might be
or might have been
and things that may never be

we trade
wings for thumbs
flight for fire

wings—any number of specialized
paired appendages

to wing a bird
prevent flight—without causing death
humans do this to birds (!)
and sometimes to each other

when Nathan was four
he awoke with a feather stuck to his skin
and thought he was turning
into a bird

time is not linear
the past exists
in the present

the mind searches in the mind
looking for affirmation
the soul completes itself
in solitude
marshals its resources
for good
for transcendence

there are many surprises
when you are drifting
turn around and the lake is silver
mercurial, protean, mutable

the heron sailing across
crosses silver, then gray
then white then gone

two bald eagles have taken up residency
in our backyard on Great Pond
what luck!
what good fortune!
I am melting

overcome with vibrational instability
overcome with a longing
I have no name for
cloudlike vaporous
that lightness of being
they talk about

yet liable at any moment
to shatter like frozen glass
into so many stars they cannot be
put in rows and counted

the heavens come down
dragging the stars along
making it easy
to put them in a jar seal it with wax
and take them with us

first and foremost
the painting is about the painting
it may not be safe to leave the house today

Eastham, MA, 2015 (Cape Cod)

(more) Thoughts while Painting

Sometimes painting is like sex
like riding a rusty bike

I am swallowed by the moon
I swallow the moon
white white white
endless
a ghostly wind

blows snow off the trees
a branch appears
A secret code
a graphic statement
intrusive yet magnificent
alerted by the retreat
of possibilities

I catch them
on the run
as they go by
the promise
elegiac
with a certain sweetness
like new honey
the color of amber in Chiapas

If it is really to be art
it must have a container
a symphonic formulation
a crescendo
a beginning and an end
some small sadness

a witness to the birth of the impossible
and the unthinkable
to the holocaust

aunts and uncles
many lost cousins
then a childhood dominated
by duck and cover

these are the ghosts
that rise from the lake

the cry of a coyote
walking across the frozen lake
it stops in the middle
standing perfectly still
frozen in space and time listening
hunger is not enough
but it is everything

I look through my grand
studio window

hours go by without trying
without a reminder of civilization
or intention

I pause
my brush swimming in air
I am thinking about the fish
that still swim at the bottom of the lake
where the water remembers
how to move

the yelp of the coyote
later in the night
has become personal
like eye contact with the gorilla
at the zoo

Eastham, MA (Cape Cod) 2015

The Blizzard
Meditation VII

great clouds of snow
like tumbleweed
tumbling across the surface
of the frozen lake
an army of ghosts
fill my emptied eyes
with angst and longing
teasing my emptied heart

if you have never seen snow
you should see it first
like this
it may cleanse your palate
for living for loving
if it does not blind you
if it does not lift you off the earth
conscripted by ghosts
carried by the tide
of the inexorable
by an explosion of angels
a figment, a phantasm
a herd of ghostly mammoths
thundering across the beginning of time

one small black bird
with little panic left
to keep it aflight
hitches a ride
on a piece of wing
left by an exploding angel

when I was very young
I caught my breath—and held it
that winged thing
flapping in its cage
of ribs and bones and cartilage
held tightly by
muscle and skin
so it could not fly away

but I was too young to know
it would not last

in time tired of my orphaned state
I began learning to love
and be loved

the blizzard is blowing through my brain
through my heart
today there is only white

Great Pond, Eastham, MA (Cape Cod) 2015

As She Lay Dying
(Memento Mori)

I crawled into my mother's bed
as she lay dying
and slipped my arms around
her tender body
wasted and waiting

it was like holding a child
she was clean and powdered
sleeping quietly
except for the soft rattle in her throat
and the tiny wheeze
in sync with the rise and fall
of her narrow chest
a cage of bone and breath
and laboring heart

the places where the comb had
raked through her shampooed hair
were like rows in the garden
ready for planting
her gown had slipped up past her knees
her thighs were a new shape
made of marble or oak
already a monument to longevity

I had said goodbye
so many times
I thought I had used up
the possibilities
but this was proving
untrue

Yom Kippur, 2015
Santa Rosa, CA; Union City, NJ

I Paint Pomegranates

Maybe it's time to paint
Another pomegranate
I paint pomegranates in the fall
I paint amaryllis
in the winter
Around xmas time

In the summer
I comb the beaches
Between Flyers
And the coast guard
For antique pottery shards
Churned up by the tides

Collective memory—past lives
May explain their blurred
Familiarity

At the height of the summer
A small army of gleaners
Who appear to be
Looking at their feet
Or digging for quahogs
With their toes

Are searching instead
For civilizations detritus
Tumbled by the pea green
Edges of the tide

I fill musky cigar boxes with them
And chinese bowls
Of discriminate longing

A thumbnail red pagoda
A tiny bothered blue bird with ruffled feathers

A horse on a mission of
Liberation from the tyranny
Of a singular motivation
Why not keep their horns you ask
Still they shed them as they emerge
through the magicians portal
That brought them

To the new world
Single file
Forgetting

I recognize the clay pipe stems
You first pointed out as bits
Of unicorn horns
But I would believe anything you told me
In those long days
we followed into moonlight
And shooting stars

They are shouting at us from
The upstairs balconies of the yellow house
Where the shards are soaking
Next to the quahogs and
The catch of the day

Time for dinner and reality

Provincetown, MA, 2017

A Little Painter in a Little Town

I am not a genius
I am not clairvoyant though
I always know who is calling
before the phone rings
A sketchy talent

What am I
Terminally curious
And lacking in certain graces
Unsettled

The canvas is still the battle ground
And my best ally
The cartilaginous tissue
Connecting these tired old bones
Keeping them standing

I mourn my cat
She taught me everything I know
And I taught her
How to be a dog
How to beg for her supper
It was our joke

A little painter
In a little town

No hail Mary for me
No last minute reprieve

An aggregate of longing and loss
Bound to pathos
Embracing the worm that
surrounds me tightly
With its silken aspirations

Forsworn each daily light
And crawled into each welcoming night

I have hidden in the corner
Of the closet—waiting for
The guests to leave

I force my cramping toes to unbend
this in itself is courageous

If I loosen my muscles
Uncurl my vertebral colonnade
If I lie flat while waiting
For the magic elixir
To deliver its promise

Arrogance flew away with youth and health
Here in the garden by the bay
On the day I returned
I found I could no longer swim

I have a studio
packed with remembrance
on boards and canvases
And plaster—like small walls

Small walls
That make a room—
Rooms that make houses
Pathways and avenues
That keep them fluid on the good days
And stagnant
On those others

What is left
To cry about

Provincetown, 2018

Love Letters (for G.C.)

He grasped my trembling hand in the dark
And folded his other hand over it
In a reassuring way
Then letting go gradually
He pulled back the gift of his fingers
pocketing his resolve

The night music whistled
Through the movie poster palms
I could hear the slap of the waves meeting the shore
And the sibilance of their return

Leading me lightly by the elbow
we walked through cobbled streets
I felt the naked black stones through my shredded sandals
I wasn't sure I was awake

We were so alike the two of us
equally pathetic and royally magnificent
When the weak sides coincided
there was no one there to take care of us
Except for a wonderful short while
when we shared our house in the redwoods
with another couple who liked to boss us around

And when their house was ready
when it ended
You and I stood face to face
forced to acknowledge the enormity of this
existential accident

The box flew open and all the angels
wore satan's masks
And all the devils whispered
Freedom at any cost

I thank you for the distant memories
bound in loves declensions
this gift of sweet sorrows
you left behind
The print by the bed in the red carpet
made by your slippers

The acrid mix—honey and nightshade
on the pillow
The tin box of letters beside the blue lamp

I had to shake us loose
The words became your body
our domain of sweet lies

You had by then a whole life
somewhere else without me
While I lived between the lines of your poetry
And mine

Provincetown, MA, 2017/2025

Fifty-three Years Ago, My Father Died at Fifty-three
Memento Mori

Fifty-three years ago
my father died at fifty-three
The world turned upside down
and didn't right itself again

The sun rose and set
We fell in love
We made babies
We made art
We voted for president
Still nobody sat in his chair

It seemed it would always be that way
Then finally without fanfare
or even acknowledgement
it was over
this silent lamentation
this somber homage

The kids played in his chair
sliding on the shiny creased leather
making it go up and down and recline
a passel of them
tumbling and laughing in Bapa's chair
with no rebuking

I can't remember exactly when it changed
when insistent priorities
and the consuming rhythm
of the commonplace
sent him up the ladder
to where the rare books are honored
and gather dust

But he still comes upon me
unexpectedly in the summer
with the sound of trimming hedges
The sweet animal smell
of the tiny white privet flowers
that float around him as he clips

56

The euphoric smell of gasoline
the raging alligator teeth
eating through the privet
In the later years
It didn't take all of Sunday anymore

On a moon filled summer's night
he stands illuminated in the doorframe
waving away the powdery moths
waiting for the Libby's peaches
can of nightcrawlers
we have pulled from the sprinkled lawn
for tomorrow's silent fishing
On the lake
That is also the sky

In midwinter
When the door flies open
Banging on its hinges
the snow blows in smelling of his tobacco
following the scraping sound
of the giant shovel at frigid dawn
making a path for the grand belching exit
of his latest jalopy

Finally a masked grandfather in the hospital
holding that mewling little thing
their wet eyes touching
And just a couple of years later
the popcorn eating grandkids press to his side
In the huge littered bed
where he has become domiciled

to hear the latest chapter
of *The Pearlmans on the Moon*
facilitated by his invention
of the anti-gravity machine
that promised all of us a new planet
To live on

Provincetown, MA 2018/2025

Main Street Movie

They are early for the evening show
but they buy their tickets
to sit in the near empty loge

The two cigarettes
that she has taken from the crumpled packet
in her father's jacket
poke out of his breast pocket
He looks smarter with his glasses

They climb the carpeted stairs
imprinted with fleur de lis
and Bauhaus geometry
descend to the edge of the abyss
and sit in the front row with
the brass colored railing

She leans over to get a precarious glimpse
of the floor below
It makes her giddy
Directly overhead
smoky dragons whirl and cavort
caught in the halo of the projector light

Directly beneath them the nasty boys
are wadding up little bits of paper
and rolling them around their tongues
with spit while the news reel plays

The matron sits in the back row
you can see her bulky shape
every time the door opens
with a harsh funnel of light
ushering in popcorn smells
and lobby chaos

The aubergine velvet curtain rises
Teenies shrieks of delight
mingle with cymbals and horns
Their cheeks are red without rouge
He leans into her
the way her Retriever does

and walks his fingers closer on the armrest
surrounding her hand with his
In the dark—his pulses quicken
She remembers sitting in this row
watching The Man in the White Suit
with Alec Guinness
her father's favorite

Down below the closing credits
for the latest redundant western
Followed by
Bugs Bunny and Woody Woodpecker
THAT'S ALL FOLKS

herald the mass exodus
of small boys pelting the last of their spit balls
at red eyed young girls who jostle in the dark
rolling around their last jawbreakers
with rainbow colored tongues

They exit arm in arm
grateful for the quiet street
and the muted colors of dusk

(Queens, NY), 2019, Cape Cod

You Said Things

You said you would like to crawl into that
Hollow that lies just above the collarbone

And live there a happy being
Curled head to tail
Roundly proud

I did not fully understand
But I understood full well

My heart leaped out of my chest
Flew with inflated wings
Clearing the colonnade
Rebounding off the ceiling

You said
You loved the hidden parts of me
The dark places
Behind my knees
Between my toes

The piggies that went to market
That climbed the himalayas
For years I dreamt of sherpas
That looked like you

You said
Someday we'll grow grizzled together
And dream with our eyes open
That beaten up old comforter
Pulled up to our scrawny necks

Looking up at the ceiling
Breathless and grinning

Provincetown, MA, 2019/2025

Natan—A Day in Paradise

It is 1956 and our first week on the kibbutz.
The Sinai war which began within days of our arrival —
    has just ended.
We are in the pomegranate orchard
being taught how to prune the trees.
It is fall but there are robust fruit hanging expectantly
and fallen to the ground — the leathery skin split open
to reveal rows of swollen crimson teeth
waiting for the army of ants who will each carry a kernel
    away on its back .
Our mouths and hands are stained like the *cohanim*
    with the purple-red juices.

Our mentor is a tall spare Englishman in faded army khaki.
His fair complexion is burnt brown and prematurely
    aged by the sun.
His hands gnarled and scarred like the tree he is deftly cutting.
He surrounds my right hand in which I grasp the shears,
with his right hand and selects a branch
leaning against me — showing me.
When he is satisfied I will not mutilate his sacred trees —
    he leaves.

Lost in paradise — I fail to notice the hush that surrounds me.
A tap on my shoulder — a whisper in my ear — brings me back,
"Don't move and be very quiet"
At my left elbow curling around a knobby branch,
its triangular head facing towards me
is a diamond patterned green and brown snake.
I have only a moment to connect to its red eyed stare
before I see its head fly off its body.

I am tackled and flung to the ground
bruised and covered with dirt.
I turn to Natan from whose open mouth
words fly out without sound like a cartoon
He picks me up and dusts me off ?"
I try to explain my errant five senses. roughly
"Why didn't you get out of the tree when I told you"
He picks up his machete and begins to wipe it off
My throat is parched. My ears are ringing.
"I didn't see the snake until it was at my elbow"

Later in the week Natan invites me with him
on his evening rounds in the fields.
I hear his tractor outside the dirt floored cabin,
climb up and sit next to him on the worn seat
that has been padded with bits of old kilims.
The little tractor hums away through the orderly fields
with an occasional cough and sputter.

Natan jumps off the tractor several times
and slides into the black night and disappears.
I strain into the darkness starting with each small noise.

The moon is rising leaving a trail of stars and celestial
        detritus in its wake.
The tractor bounces along at a pretty fast clip when without
warning we stop again.
There are a number of dark shapes moving towards us—
        speaking Arabic.
"They want us to drink coffee with them."
Now the moon is high in the sky and nearly full.
The smell of coffee mixes not unpleasantly
with the smell of animal dung and burning wood.
Smoke rises curling around the cutouts
of several camels behind the main tent.
Behind them the fields stretch rhythmically
out to the edge of the softened Nazareth dunes.

We sit on a red and black striped rug in the smaller tent,
drinking strong dark coffee that singes your tongue
        and coats your teeth—
very sweet out of little white cups,
while an old man in a white kafiah and his handsome son
offer many many camels and sheep for my purchase.
Natan informs our hosts that I am taken.
"You are a lucky man." the old Bedouin says,
*"May you be blessed with many children with hair of flames
like their beautiful mother."*

The now gracious moon appears to be following our return.
"A sign of good fortune," Natan offers.
I must find a way of thanking him for beheading the viper
        and saving my life.
He nods and smiles and kisses me briefly on the lips.

Not long after my moonlit tractor ride our group moved
        to Jerusalem.
We are there less than a week—when we are ordered
        back to the kibbutz.

Meeting the tender at the gate—we are brought immediately
    to the infirmary
and asked if we had had our polio shots.
Only those who have already had two shots will be given
    a third.

If you have had all three shots you will be given a booster.
The medic takes me aside and asks me if I want a shot.
He does not tell me why he has singled me out.

Someone on the kibbutz, they finally tell us—has contracted
    Bulbar Polio.
Natan—He is in isolation and cannot be visited.
He passed away within the week.
There is a marker on the grassy knoll above the kibbutz that
    I looked for in 2000.

Israel, 2000
Provincetown, 2019/2025

The Cossacks Are Coming
Memento Mori—Grandma Jenny/Jean Stark

My brother had departed in a whirr after
ferrying me there promising to return in a week or so
The grandkids were taking turns
watching over their adored *Mamma Jenny*
In her last days sleeping on the floor by her bed

Jenny now over ninety and legally blind
She still drank black coffee all day
A potent elixir kept warm at the back of the stove

Her meals were delivered but rarely eaten
Her pals brought her pastries and soft fruits
she ate in small bites
pulling off bits of danish with two fingers
and swallowing them with coffee
She saw mostly shadows and outlines
yet she could pick a straight pin from the carpet
and cautioned me about my bare feet

She was at the center of a bunch of old ladies
that had been together at the *Golden Ages*
for decades—now dwindling
There were four *peer counselors* remaining
One, a nun who spoke yiddish visited almost every day
The rest met around her bed weekly
Sometimes they played canasta or rummy
on a black lacquer bed table perched on her lap
She often drifted off but they didn't seem to notice

Jenny was born in Ukraine in a shtetl near Minsk
She came to the US in 1917
married to Sam by *shidduch*
so they could travel to the new world together
He was an actor with the yiddish theatre
and very handsome
When he impregnated one of the *Polishikas*
In her sweatshop
Jenny sent him packing

Now a single mom with two children
she lived in a tenement on the lower East Side
Where she copied the latest fashions

64

from windows on fifth avenue
And sold patterns and samples
To the discounters

She was always very political and socially conscious
a communist until Czechoslovakia
In her later years in California
she was an activist with the progressive party

In the fifties McCarthy tried to have her deported
But her second husband had a bad heart
and so they let her stay

When we lived in Florida
the FBI in dark suits and dark glasses
sat sweating for weeks in a parked car across the street
from her tiny stucco house
with an orange tree on the front lawn

We sat at her kitchen table by the window
having grilled cheese and iced tea
and watched them watching us

While I took my turn at her beside
she remembered that I could cook
And made a decision to eat all the foods
that had been forbidden her
Like meatballs and spaghetti
and strawberry shortcake

After a bit we settled into a pattern
Sometimes she would get up for morning coffee
But mostly I brought it to her bedside
while we planned the day's menu

In the late afternoon
we shared a glass of sherry
from the bottle that had been her one request
Harvey's Bristol Myers she called it
And beating her old misshapen slippered feet
on the floor next to her bed
she reproduced the sound
of the thundering hooves of the cossacks
approaching her village

And then resting her beautiful
head on the propped up bed pillows
continued the story of hiding in the haystacks
with her cousin while the village
filled with smoke

Provincetown, 2019/2025

The Dark Night of the Soul

The Essential Image
There must be one
Like a nova
With a congregation of smaller suns

Tripping on its hem
Falling into the stratosphere
It's heel caught in conjecture

It is after all a non thing
A black hole
Although now we are obliged to
Look at the darn things seriously

This Abbreviation

A pinpoint of darkness
In the deep part of my brain
A moment of trauma perhaps
A bit of sand from the
Sea of memory

I hid behind the winter coats in the hall closet
Wrapped in my mother's moutan
When I was a wee girl and there were visitors
In the forbidden pink living room

At school I rarely spoke
I mostly looked out the scarred windows
That seemed to ripple in the wind

Trying to steady my legs
That so ached to be out and away
They would not stay still

I may never have one
singular-transcendent moment
Or they may never find it
So perfectly buried
Between sheets of foolscap—another perfect word

The sun goes to rest
Behind the dunes
I watch it sink
Feeling the sucking of the planet

I should mend any fences
That are still left

Forlorn—a clever word
It forces the mouth into empty kisses
It sounds right

Let life empty penultimately
And fill up slowly again
Sliding on tears and promissory notes
The ways of the world
Don't change so much
After all
They shift and sort
And fall off the earth
While other parts
Grow toward its center

Nebulas collide—collude
And deals are made in late night phone calls
Between crooked kings

Provincetown, 2024

My eyes play tricks

Do I hallucinate
The side of that house
Across the street
Now goes around the corner
And I can see the back
From the front
Do I think I am Picasso

I live for these moments
a reward
Passed along through

A barrage of sequential encoding

Our inheritance
Lacking only one or two small degrees
Of resting before continuing
In reverse
Open to mutation and dalliance
Open to massive joy and relentless tragedy
On one slim line

The time between
A millisecond
Am I losing or gaining
My mind that is
My selfhood
And the avenue to simple pleasure

Provincetown, 2024

Winter
meditation I

I am surrounded by
stained shingled houses
that rattle with emptiness
and gray branches
that have forgotten summer

but in the pink twilight
The red foxes
Come to play
And eat the abandoned apples
In the empty yard

Provincetown, 2024/2025

Winter
meditation II

Where there is true knowledge
And also where knowledge
Has succumbed to whimsy and magic
this is also true
in another way
Through another portal

How did we arrive here
How do we survive here
At the end of everything
Where the tail bites the head/
The head the tail
The ouroboros
Another winter almost done

Provincetown, 2024/2025

71

The Trees in Winter
meditation III

The Trees in Winter
Stand bare and unabashed
It is their turn
To show their attenuated loveliness
Their loyalty
No artifice of greenery
They grace the roadside
In solidarity

I frame them in my mind
For later
In the studio

The winter vista
Like the emptiness
The nobility of the desert
echo my singularity
My solitude
Their sameness persuades
and comforts me
Mirrors reflected in mirrors

The army of voices tangled in
brooding cerebration
give way to
the grace of the empty mind

Stripped of foliage
Naked and content

2019, Provincetown
Festschrift for Keith Althaus (80th birthday) 2025

When the First Bird Sings
Memento Mori for Jerry Schwartz
(my first lost best friend)

Between the angels and the beast
An essay about free will dawns

The road to enlightenment
is without effort
advancing with age
Completing itself

Embracing solitude
choosing emptiness
forgoing passion
But there are the times
It catches us unaware

Mostly after dark
When the moon hides
Or just before dawn

When the first bird sings

Provincetown, 2023/2025

The Wadi
The Yellow Dog

This morning when I walked in the desert by the caves
I met a young woman walking with a yellow dog
She is distracted paying him little attention
He stops every ten feet or so to lick the morning dewfall
caught in the craters of the rocks
that line the dry stream bed

We could be on the moon—some distant planet or star
except for the sound of the camel bells
The yellow dog turns and smiles
wags his handsome tail—Its fringes a darker color

trail on the sand collecting thorny bits and burrs
to be addressed later in front of the evening fire
As the celestial orbs exchange places
In the darkening sky

His mistress retying her *keffiyeh*
in a quick and clever way around her head
pulls herself from her reverie
and acknowledges my presence

I respond to the oh so slight lift of her dark brows
Boker Tov—Good morning

The yellow dog with a patient expression
turns to the sound of the camel bells
and moves on sniffing the air
making little whining sounds at the back of his throat
accompanied by great jaw stretching yawns

We have crossed this southern section of the wadi
the view from my studio window
and continue north together
Just above us moving in a snaking line
up and around the side of the dune
are the camels and their herders

The youngest dromedaries are at the end of the line
The white ones are especially beautiful—
I have often had fantasies of adopting one
The smallest whitey calf just weeks old

appears to be managing with a little help—
from the boy and his dog who keep him on the path

Behind the youngsters with the knobby knees—
placing one cautious hoof in front of the other
A bearded elder cow pulls up the rear bellowing
The yellow dog barks back in a contiguous
stream of invectives

The herdsmen join the fracas—*yallah yallah*
An echo carries the guttural sound aloft
and repeats and repeats it as it winds through the wadi
all the way to the Dead Sea in the morning
and back again at dusk

The camels who have begun to smell the promise of water
pick up their pace grunting and bellowing
The color of the sky changes subtly without notice
until a bolt of lightning and a clap of thunder
awaken the landscape—

We have become so used to drought—
that we have stopped thinking about rain
In the event that it comes down heavily
we must all run to the caves for cover

Some of the caves are quite deep
littered with the detritus of refuge seekers since time began—
It is said that whole armies have retreated here

The Bedouins and their camels carry their world with them
and can wait out the storm in the caves
But the three of us will be trapped
by the wadi filling with water

Lightning, thunder
a plague of hail stones the size of walnuts
fall on our heads and pelt our backs—
A few odd moments of silence paralyze us
before the first tentative drops fall

They hit the ground accompanied by a deafening clap of
thunder—
Lightning zig zags its way to the molten center of the earth
And then the biblical rain heralded by a steamy cloud
rising up from the sand—

and the smell of ozone is quickly followed
by raindrops the size of jelly beans
Bellowing camels and screaming calves

join the chorus of bells and barking dogs
Cracks of lightning illuminate the hellish thickened sky

The yellow dog sets the pace and leads the way
We run behind him pulling in painful searing breaths
Through the wadi to the road
I can see the studio
We are almost there

Arad, Israel, 2000/2018; Provincetown, 2025

Desiderata

What a lovely word
from desire
The meaningless things we desire
pursue desultory
or with passion
Aimless versus pointed
versus committed
versus focused
versus work
versus leisure
Dolce fa niente
Sometimes it is sweet
to do nothing
and want nothing
I have climbed to the top of a sycamore
I can feel the chosen branch
sway and bend beneath me
I have chosen this tree
for the sound of its name
like the sibilant hiss
of the leaves
whispering to each other
telling each other
the secrets of trees

Will I live long enough
to renegotiate the secrets
of childhood
the ready knowledge
the certainty
without trying
without asking
There is no one to ask

Desiderata
I read it in an old book
I wasn't sure what it meant
what part of desire
or all of it
Ah but the sound of it
foreign on the palette
yet easy

I roll it around on my tongue
It shapes my mouth
with each syllable
My lips coming together
and parting again

It wants to be a song
a celebration of hedonism
A Tango

Montclair, NJ, 2005; Provincetown 2025

A Few Moments that Are Really Mine
New digs (meditation)

The restless moon
Rising through the silver night
fills the little window behind my head
I can see its twin reflected
In the shiny new faucet

Land of crickets
and privacy
I am alone in my kitchen
The remaining dishes
soaking
I rearrange the cabinet
Tomorrow I will probably put it back
The way it was
An agony of pleasure
The small measured things

Provincetown, 2025

Memento Mori

Each Day (after Rambam—Maimonides) for Rico

Each day that we live
We die a little
In the embers of night
In the smoke of dreams

At the end of each morning
When the sun has stopped climbing
The angels gather together
To borrow its rays

At dusk and at dawn
With every stroke of the brush
With each word
each sentence
every question mark
And parenthesis

And everytime I
turn out the light
And check to see
That the black dog
lies at my bedside

Who watches
and sits at the side
of Michael the archangel

Who sits at the side
Of God
Goodnight Rico
Tomorrow is another day
Chasing turkeys in the yard

> *(Chapter 20 of the Book of Enoch mentions seven holy angels who watch, that often are considered the seven archangels: Michael, Raphael, Gabriel, Uriel, Saraqael, Raguel, and Remiel.)*

> *(Of course science in Rambam's (Maimonides) time did not speak of DNA in the same way that we do, but his phrase "God has placed in the sperm a formative force shaping the limbs" reflects contemporary science as he understood it. He sees no contradiction between the languages of science and religion.)*
> *Provincetown, 2024/2025*

Bee Cottage
Memento Mori

You will love it here—she said
we reserve it for newlyweds
don't mind the bees they won't bother you
the one circling your head
hangs in the air a moment
buzzing in place
then moves on

The pages in the sketchbook you carry
say little and the new colors wait unopened
on the green enamel table

you read a mystery
a Doris Lessing and then another
an Agatha Christie
in a yellow garden chair
made of woven plastic and aluminum
at the edge of the pond

a big floppy hat—shades your eyes
later you walk around the pond—not much more
than a mud hole really carrying it

Green algae floats geographically
like lunar barges
manned by
twenty or so
species of frogs
(Tom, the gardener can name about five)
a persuasive chorus
as now the moon rises

Your new husband is still not home
the dinner of his favorites
waits at the back of the stove
The Zorsia pokes at and tickles your feet
you sit again in the yellow chair
watching the clouds parade across the moon
and wake slapping mosquitos

There are lights on in the cottage
It's time to broil the steak

and remove the foil
from the baked potato
take the salad from the half-frig
and sit across from each other
at the rickety table
knees bumping

The bees hum all through the night
on the other side of the bedroom wall
you lie awake in the big honeymoon bed
he snores softly
sometimes breaking the rhythm
to snort and catch his breath

The fourth or fifth day
after you circle the pond
pulling your feet in their flip-flops
out of the sodden grass
every few steps—slow going
you have that Alice in Wonderland feeling again

On the way back for no reason
you detour from the slate path
choosing the mud and grass
that goes around the back of the cottage
the wall is black with bees from roof to floor

bees continue to arrive from all directions
they are everywhere and deafening
You hold your ears

In the morning
After your husband
Returns to work
Your father comes to get you

Provincetown, 2015/2025

* alternative final ending

I don't think I can stand one more day

my father comes to pick me up
his hug is fierce
his faded blue eyes are wet

he fires my new husband
and sends us back to school

Provincetown, 2025

82

Memento Mori for H.P.
Spider and Isadora

Yes it's true
I ran away to the Russian River
with a former student—in 1972

He was very tall and lanky
(You could barely see him sideways)
With gangly arms and legs
and narrow hips—I called him Spider

He hailed from Little Rock
the capital of Arkansas
and spoke without a drawl when he wanted to
But I loved that lazy humid sound—
Talk southern I would say
It may have made one think he was slow witted
But that was hardly the case

As a teen he had taught himself yoga
from a pilfered library book
And still had an active daily practice
including standing on his head for hours

He inherited his waist long blue black hair
from his Cherokee Granny
And his height and eye color from the Norsemen
on his father's side
On the night of our exhibition
in a downtown gallery
He drank too much
and pulled his paintings from the walls
And later that evening
He slashed his wrists
though not deep enough to die
I brought him penicillin and clean bandages
for the next few apologetic weeks

On the nights we could get away
We wore our cowboy boots
in dingy country bars
in the next town over

83

Drank Southern Comfort and
listened to Linda Ronstadt

Often in the afternoons he brought his little girl over
to swim with my little girls in the pool
overhung with native trees
covered with orchids and bromeliads
They giggled together at the shallow end
while we drank sweet tea and ate boiled peanuts

We went downtown to see the Isadora movie
when it came out
I knew everything about her
And had absorbed her wonderful dances
that seemed so simple
But left you in a sweat

I hated the movie
It was Vanessa Redgrave
She didn't fit the part
Isadora wasn't elegant in that way
And they didn't understand her artistry her politics
And her pleading sensuality

I was so upset
Why didn't they hire Me
Why didn't they cast Me
I kept repeating—Attracting some attention
He slipped his arm around my shoulder
leaning in towards me
he had a wonderful scent
Bergamot I think
And whispered in my ear to calm me
But you didn't audition he repeated
Offering up a sobering kind of logic

Provincetown, 2017

Flaunting Solitude

The first snow has turned to rain
in the rueful hours

I have been watching it
through the scarred and grimy panes
give up and become water again
and slide down my steps
and puddle in the patio below
I plead it is not yet time to begin the real winter
but it is coming
ringing in my bones

why have I returned
to this narrow place
what sins to undo
what heat to reimagine

come down from the lofty peg
you prescribe
and play with the foxes
in the perfect pink twilight

Return to Provincetown, 2015/2025

Creation/Intention

Who am I
and why am I
Why was I positioned here
on this glorious earth
And why am I alone
with no companion breath
To remind me
who I am

Listening to the separate hummings
joining symphonically with harmonic intention
sheltered by the skin of the night

Gathering itself together from
bits of ether that lie between
the particles of dust and detritus

The stuff that comes together
like a golem or an angel
made of the fits and starts
of lost intention
of mislaid nobility

The declensions of time—and heart
alchemically supported
by the sun's distilled rays slipping through
The rift between the heavens and the earth

God has not yet invented a conscience
thus we are obliged to keep it all going
By embracing the molecular movement
By riding on the backs of subatomic particles
Through black holes and giving birth to reflected light

Possibilities abound

Provincetown, 2024/2025

Memento Mori
for Edie—my beloved sister

Play Ball
(Edie and the Softball Team at the Y)

We played softball at the Y.W.C.A. in Jamaica Queens
It was about thirty minutes away—
down Main Street to Jamaica Avenue.
We could see the gathering group
in front of the beat up old building
even before the bus let us off on the corner.

They watched us approach *"the last mile"*
Not a single smile or greeting cracked the waiting pack.

Edie had persuaded me to join the team
and did her best to coach me.
But—I was everyone's last choice
The worst player on the team.

Standing there alone as they made their choices.
Walking in silence to the dead pan group
that were stuck with me.

I had decided to quit
when E persuaded me to come—one last time
and guaranteed I would get a hit . . .
I agreed—one last time.

The Y.W. was housed in an ancient stucco building
near the downtown section of Jamaica Queens.
Demographically mixed but weighted heavily
with really big strong neighborhood girls
who practically lived in the broken down gym
A murkey funky old place
smelling always of feet and mildew.

87

If the ball hit the wall bits and pieces
of peeling paint and plaster ended up on the floor
making it dangerously slick and gritty.
We suspected that some of the girls
were deliberately accelerating
the disintegration of the gym.
A ball that hit the wall causing
the plaster to rain down invariably elicited
a more than warranted amount of cheering.

On my "last night" at the YW
Edie gave me a few new batting tips
While she managed to score the position
of pitcher on the opposite team.
"Just swing the bat as I showed you
and leave it to me," she said.

On the first pitch I came closer to hitting
the ball—than I had ever done before.
The bat connected with the outer covering of the ball
and stopped it dead in the air for a few milliseconds
Before dropping it—and splitting it open at my feet.

On the second pitch, the bat connected full on with the ball
that went into the side lines, a foul.
Still—both tries were better than ever before
and I was feeling flushed—confident.

On the third pitch, Edie threw it directly to my bat again
AND—I hit it back with all the Jedi force I could muster.
The ball and bat connected with a thunderous whack

Traveling on a determined vertical trajectory
to the ceiling of the gym—connecting squarely
with a top hat fixture—with such colossal impact
that it not only blew the massive eggplant shaped bulb
raining glass down on all the assembled stunned ball players
but knocking out the power for the whole gym.

The game was canceled
and both of us were kicked off the team

Provincetown, 2017/2025

Memento Mori (the post holocaust years)
Death

Grandpa died when I was three. We went by train to Detroit to fetch him home for the burial and to take Grandma back with us. I never asked about it. I did not have the right questions.

Did we go on a long echoing train ride in the tubular dark with lights like mislaid stars going off and on when I was a very little girl?

My nose pressed hard against the cold window, Edie warm and silent beside me, Harry across the aisle sandwiched between Mom and Dad.

In the growing up years, I often dreamt of dark trains racing through the night, hearing the echo of my cries—blindly reaching for my sister.

Once a year on the anniversary of my grandfather's death we visited his grave. Shoulder to shoulder and elbow to elbow in a cramped car packed like sardines

We drove for many eons on an endless highway shouldered by vivid fall foliage—complaining and bickering endlessly. Grandma crowded in the rumble seat with us drying her red rimmed eyes coming and going.

At the cemetery we waited gracelessly in the car or standing by the car door while Celia found her way through the granite markers with the mysterious stones perched on the top

prostrated herself on the grassy mound in front of the one marked with Grandpa's name and wailed in a deep and primitive way. We watched them go as they got smaller and smaller disappearing through a big black scrolled iron gate

and reappearing again over the little grassy knoll that separated us from the inconsolable small woman who didn't seem to belong to us anymore.

We didn't talk much about death, during these post holocaust years imagining heaven as a separate world where everything was the same as here but different because God and the angels were there and you got everything you desired.

We didn't dare talk about death above a whisper—lest you wake up the malach hamavet (the angel of death.)

By the same token you never paid or received compliments to your family without a lot of spitting (pttoo, pttoo) or saying kinahora (to ward off the evil eye.) If things were going too well, if life was too good, if the bride was too beautiful the Cossacks and the Nazis were just around the corner.

Six—million Jews—gone

I heard about "the camps" in the third grade at the Yeshiva of Central Queens alluding to some of our teachers who looked gray and had numbers on their arms and were missing fingers.

I didn't visit a cemetery or attend a funeral until my father's death in 1965.

Provincetown, summer 2022/2025

You Said Things (Promises)

You said you would like to crawl into
that hollow that lies just above the collarbone

And live there a happy being
Curled head to tail
Roundly proud

I did not fully understand
But I understood full well

My heart leapt out of my chest
Flew with inflated wings
Clearing the colonnade
Rebounding off the ceiling

You said
You loved the hidden parts of me
The dark places
Behind my knees
Between my toes

The piggies that went to market
That climbed the himalayas
For years I dreamt of sherpas
That looked like you

You said
Someday we'll grow grizzled together
And dream with our eyes open
That beaten up old comforter
Pulled up to our scrawny necks
Looking up at the ceiling
Breathless and grinning

2019/2025, Provincetown

Waiting (dream)

An empty shape white on white
But I think I see a black slip of a shadow
on a moving stairway
A kite winder
zig-zagging across the snow hatted hill

A faint silhouette against
the bald blue sky
I am not convinced
But I am still hoping it is you

The shape of your mouth barely moving
parched by the dry air and the waiting
But you are still too far away
to be certain If it is you

The sun at mid-sky
the shadow at his feet
or where his feet might be
seems to be growing
My eyes slitted like a serpent
I see him but only because
I am looking so hard
hoping not to see him
turn away

Soon it will be too late
His long stride making ladders in the snow
And I would have to wait another day
An eternity

Provincetown, 2023/2025

Why Have the Foxes

why have the foxes
become so bold
let's find out
about things
you whispered
your breath warm
against my ear
so long ago

let's find out before
they take you from me
is it this place and
the way you looked
at me then
I never asked for this

but still
the red fox
crossing commercial street
in the daylight
must stand for something
why have the foxes
become so bold

in the wilderness
behind route six
a slender vixen
is awakened by her barking kits
she draws them close
to suckle

we saw a white fox
last winter on great pond
against the snow
I thought I knew
its secret
for that short moment
when we were both
foxes by the lake
with barely an outline

Provincetown, winter 2016/2025

Old Friend (for Michael C.)

your eyes are fine and kind
older and kinder
than the last time
than the lost time
your heart compressed
holds family, old friends and lovers

a smooth stone
at the bottom of a river
of regret—who can help it
a sweet pain remains

with one noble foot in the past
memory hardened and polished by time

gleaning compassion
in the fields—in the yards
in the zoos of mercy
in the velvet halls
of the aristocrat—the artist

I applaud where you are
having learned a thing or two
about noblesse
you save your old friends

holding tight to the smallest thing
the careless have let go

there you will sit to the right of god
ordering the angels about
Mikael—Mikael

> *Provincetown, 2021*
> *Happy Birthday*
> *September 3, 2025*

Swallow the Moon

A curious wind blows snow off the trees
a branch appears like a coded message

I awake dragging a reluctant dream
watching the retreat of possibilities
an army of afterthought
frayed at the collar
down on its heals

a promise—brittle with time lost
yet tinged with a certain sweetness
like new honey
the color of amber in Chiapas

If it is to be art
it must have a container
a symphonic formulation
a hesitation
a held breath
a joining
a crescendo
a finale
a lingering sadness

It must forbear the impossible
the unthinkable
aunts and uncles eaten by shadow
lost cousins mirror back at us
Already slipping away
whispers corrupt the silence
affidavits—what could that mean

then by McCarthy and threatened deportation
Grandma Jenny who only wanted
the world to take care of its poor and hungry

then by *duck and cover* and further ignominies
And a world that would blow itself up
In a twisted minute

These are my thoughts
painting the lingering shadows
hearing the cry of the coyote
on it's morning walk across the lake

it's dog outline mirrored on the ice
It's solitude a slip of genetics—

hunger is not enough—but it is everything
he will swallow the moon

Still the fish swim at the bottom of the pond
where the water remembers how to move

The yelp of the coyote later in the night
is familiar and personal
like eye contact with the gorilla
at the zoo

In the morning a cardinal
lands on the deck
flat footed
feathers fluted against the chill
blood red on the snow
flaunt your biretta
in this monochrome

Eastham, 2014; Provincetown, 2025

Memento Mori (Grandpa Harry)
Riding Horses in Detroit and Coming to America

In the winter my dad's friends at school
went out on weekends to a ranch not far from the city
They had discovered they could exercise the animals for free
Dad continued to beg for months to go
but Grandpa didn't take his interest very seriously
In the old country horses pulled carts and plows

Fed up with all his begging and pleading
My grandfather finally relented
One bright crisp early winter day found them
in their latest model Ford
on the road that lead to the outskirts of the city
It was my dad's birthday

Grandpa was in good spirits
encouraging his son to tell him all about the ranch
and the horses
They were almost there
Dad was terribly excited eager to show off the stables
There were two horses to choose from
that freezing morning

Did Grandpa want to ride
Oh no, he would watch his son
There was a horse Dad had set his eyes on
Grandpa had suggested the mare
Who was smaller and more sedate
But Dad chose the bigger horse

It was snorting and tossing its head
You could see its great dragon breath on the air
the rippling across its skin.
The groom saddled up the gelding
With the gallery glued to his every move
Dad mounted it with a leg up from his father
and grabbed the reins ready to go

The horse was snorting and pawing the ground
Going nowhere standing like stone
Grandpa went up to the horse ignoring Dad's warning
He was making an odd sound between his teeth
The horse lifted his proud head turned

and looked at Grandpa
Grandpa made the sound again
And the horse walked steadily around the paddock
picking up steam

Every so often it would rise up on its hind legs
snort and whinny probably just happy to be out of its stall
Dad's hat had blown off and his longish hair
he always hated getting a haircut
blew across his reddened cheeks.

He looked excited and a little anxious
(not scared to death as Grampa later told it)
They rode around the paddock several times
The next time the horse reared up
Dad almost fell off backwards
but managed to get back in the saddle
and keep going.

Grandpa took a moment off
from blowing on his chilled fingers
to whistle to the horse
who came trotting proudly back to the gate
Maybe that's enough he said

I'm doing fine Dad replied
What do you know about horses anyway
or something sassy like that.
Get down off that thing and I'll show you
Dad grinning replied quietly
You think you can ride him

What happened next is hard to describe
although I made my Dad tell it over and over again
then and for years to come
No sooner had Grandpa landed in the saddle
he was on the ground again
and then back in the saddle with ease
leaping onto the horse and then to the ground
over and over again
Finally remaining on the ground

Dad thought the show was over
when Grandpa climbed up and sat on the fence next to him
The horse continued circling the paddock
Then Grandpa whistled and the horse ran by
close enough so that Grampa could mount him on the run

He repeated his former trick of jumping on and off the horse
one time even landing backwards on his rump
and holding on to his tail.
Dad closed his gaping jaw long enough
to laugh until his sides hurt

The horse seemed to know the program and the joke
When Grandpa walked away as if the fun was over
he butted Grampa in the rear
Grampa grabbed his tail and within seconds
was in the saddle

There seemed no end of tricks
this Russian Jew from the shtetl
and this American quarter horse could do

Grandpa laughed and chuckled to himself
all the way home
While Dad nonplussed and more than a bit annoyed
bit down on his teeth,
crossed his arms across his chest and said nothing.

Dad stayed angry for quite a while
If Grampa had this secret
what else about his past had he hidden from his children

Finally he had to ask
And the long time buried story emerged bit by bit
His dad and his brothers (the lost uncles)
regularly traveled by horseback across the mountains
and acquired wild Arabian horses breaking them on the trip
home
after some further training they sold them to the Cossacks
But what about all the tricks

While they were training the horses who caught on very quickly
they would get into contests
doing more and more difficult riding tricks.
Sometimes they would gather a crowd
and make a little side money
Then he got into a fight with a Cossack
who refused to pay for the horses.
He said if Grampa beat him in a fair fight that he would pay.

The family desperately needed the money.
Grampa was strong and a good fighter
when it looked like he was winning the Cossack pulled a knife
Grampa kicked it out of his hand and knocked him
unconscious

Then Grandpa took the horses
and sold them on his way out of the country
He swam the Volga river (as the story goes)

It took a year to get on a boat
and come to America.

Montclair, NJ, 2018
Provincetown, MA, 2025

Jenny and Celia

Gramma Celia at the beach looked like a Bedouin wrapped in robes and blankets covering every inch of her lily white body. On her nose, over the protective white stuff that she also wore smeared across her cheeks and any other parts of her that were likely to escape her burqa and be exposed to the dreaded sun, she added a plastic nose cap for extra protection.

Jenny and Celia were at war from the minute their children married each other. They both came from approximately the same neighborhood. Jenny from a farming area near Odessa and Celia from a shtetl near Minsk. Jenny was a "peasant" and Celia was the daughter of a Rav—a rabbi. Jenny was a communist, a secular Jew who observed the holidays and life cycles. She spoke Russian and Yiddish and heavily accented English and was literate in all three.

Celia, who came from a traditional family, spoke only Yiddish (a little Polish and less Russian) and English. She could read the Forverts (The Jewish Daily Forward in Yiddish) but I don't think she could write very well in any language and her reading of anything other than Yiddish or really simple English was halting. Jenny was a worldly woman who continued to support her family and have boyfriends after divorcing her p hilandering husband when he impregnated the "polishaka" seamstress in her sweat shop (that replicated couturier fashions).

Celia ran a tiny luncheonette, candy store in Detroit where husband Harry worked for Ford motor having been recruited straight off the boat. After Harry died in his early sixties—Celia moved near us and worked for Lofts making candy for a while and then came to live with us and ate white food, farina and fish potato soup that had long ago stopped containing fish and occasionally noodles and cottage cheese.

Jenny stuck it out with the communist party marching against a variety of causes advocating for support of the Lincoln Brigade in the Spanish Civil war until her son, my uncle Dave ran away to join up. And later joined Mother's March for Peace and the progressive party during her California years. She officially resigned from the party after the Prague Spring. But was still hunted down by McCarthy in the fifties and only just avoided deportation by the fact that her then husband (Jack Stark) had a life threatening heart condition. She was a lifetime follower of Adele Davis and made us meatloaf with "veet joims," wheat germs

I found this article while checking on the exact title for the Yiddish newspaper.

"100 Years Ago in the Forward"

"Forsyth Street resident Feige Gabeh, 20, disappeared this week and is rumored to be in hiding with Joe Shuster, a former border in her parents' home who also disappeared from his wife and two children. Shuster and Gabeh, who knew each other from the Old Country, were having an affair under the noses of Gabeh's parents, who took Shuster in because he was a landsman. When Shuster's wife and children came over from Russia, he moved out of the Gabeh's apartment and into a room on Allen Street. Gabeh continued to visit him and became close friends with his wife, too. But neighbors began to talk, saying that Gabeh and Shuster were too close and that it would end badly, which it apparently has."

Jersey City, 2020; Provincetown, 2024

Lost at Coney Island

When I was four, maybe almost five years old my wonderful Grandma Jenny, Pauline's feisty, activist mother whom we called Mommy Jenny or Jenny but never Grandma took me to Coney Island Beach and lost me. We all, my sibs and I that is —loved Mommy Jenny. As an adult I often referred to her as "the Permitter". In the lives of all five of us Jenny (Jean Chriss Stark) took the grandmotherly role of provider of unconditional love and support. We adored her.

It was an incredibly bright and sunny early summer day. There was a light breeze that played with the hems of the flowered summer dresses of the boardwalk promenaders but not enough to blow the straw boaters and sailor hats off their beaux's pomaded heads.

Acrid ocean smells fought with the powerful sweetness of cotton candy. Cotton Candy, what magic—from cone gathering inception to the forbidden consumption (forbidden by my mother who worried about our teeth and later about our weight). I watched the magic accruing while Mommy Jenny talked to the vendor. She knew everyone. And most of them spoke in the funny and endearing way she did. "Efter lunch we'll hev some", she told me. I was willing to wait.

I knew she had brought my favorite foods in the string bag she carried looped around her wrist. I loved grilled cheese sandwiches, even cold, even when the bread had gone soft and the cheese rubbery. I had watched her packing our lunch earlier while I ate breakfast at the shiny kitchen table in her Brooklyn apartment. French Toast with marmalade. Now I was sitting on the little fold up stool Jenny carried in her satchel that had the straw roses on it.

I was in my new blue (my favorite color) bathing suit with an oversized white tee shirt over it to protect my pale skin from sun damage. My nose was covered with the prerequisite white stuff. And my arms and legs had been well smeared with Coppertone for kids. Jenny had dark skin; she had patiently explained to me and did not need the same protection from the sun. She was brown as a berry, had dark hair and dark eyes like my mother, though Pauline's skin was reddish and she freckled in the summer.

Earlier, my very popular grandmother and I had walked together to the edge of the surf, stopping often along the way to say hi—and put our feet in the icy water. Then we very bravely walked in very slowly up to my knees with the surf hitting the backs of our legs. Then she lifted me up by my arms and we walked a few additional feet. We had a game I loved. We huddled down together waiting for the surf yelling , Here it comes!, Here it comes! getting louder and louder as the waves approached. Here it comes!

Then she lifted me up and out of the water by my thin white arms that were growing colonies of goosebumps—just at the exact moment the waves reached us,dipping me back in the water again in time for a small wave and then up again and then back and up again many times. Here it comes! as I giggled and screamed with joy. The waves at the edge of the surf were small but looking up I could see the breakers in the distance crashing against the waiting ocean.

If I looked, I could not stop looking so I tried to keep my head down and follow the small waves. Afterwards we walked hand in hand along the cool strip of packed sand and across the warm sugary stuff that got between your toes, to the boardwalk where we sat on a green bench and cleaned the sand off our feet with the edge of a striped towel. I was putting on a new pair of sandals bought earlier that week and Jenny helped me close the buckles.

I looked up gratefully and that's when I saw the cotton candy. "You can have some after lunch . . ." I was glued to the big glass box that held the machine that spun the sugar into pink magic. I circled the box with my nose pressed to the glass around and around and when I finally looked up I didn't see my grandma. I continued to circle the box stopping to ask the cotton candy man over and over again . . . "Where is my grandma? Where is my grandma?" She was gone. I couldn't find her.

I walked along the boardwalk saying her name over and over again. Mommy Jenny, Mommy Jenny, Mommy Jenny. Then I was running and crying Mommy Jenny, Mommy Jenny and screaming Mommy Jenny until I caught my sandal on a raised board and fell and skinned my knee. The shock of falling squelched my tears while a small crowd assembled around me. They were all talking at once. And I couldn't separate the words.

I wasn't crying anymore even though my knee was bleeding freely onto the boardwalk and making a small puddle. Where's your mom? What's your name? What's your name? Finally a big man in a white jacket picked me up and asked, "Whatsa matta kid? Cat got your tongue?"—And carried me to the first aid station. A boardwalk cop in a blue uniform brought me lemonade AND ice cream. But the cat had my tongue. The words were in my head but somewhere far away . . . the loudspeaker was announcing . . . If you are missing a child please come to the first aid station . . . and then I saw Momma Jenny running towards me. The string bag swinging from her wrist.

Jersey City, NJ, 2014

Playing God (A Matter of Physics)

For and with Nathan Raven—Natan (Hebrew נָתָן) Reuben or Reuven (Hebrew רְאוּבֵן) (my grandson) (student of physics and mathematics—artist and poet)

Imagining creation (losely) some thoughts about duality (the present) invention and newness—past and future

(the inner life—carved as it were from the matrix of being—of musing and deep thinking— learning and intuition—feeling and prophesy—longing and love)

We seek to be consistently human in the way of all other humans—yet unique— unchanged yet mutable—each moment each act experienced within the physical and psychical world already belonging to the past the moment uttered...

Doing is the smoke of being (neither and both) As for the past —in this moment and already gone—it lives briefly—a hair's breath—during our lifetime—and forever in our remembering—

in each scratch or stain on a wall in each footstep in the mud or sand, in each recorded and unrecorded act and every utterance carried by the wind. In every wave that makes it to shore and revives itself through retreating and gathering and advancing and retreating and gathering and advancing . . . we are creating intention . . . unintentionally IT exists without duality, recreating itself without effort or will . . . Awareness without comment—expectation without divisiveness—without longing

after billions of years of random sequestration—all is contained without a container. Emptiness that shapes a space —is profound.

Profound understanding is found and lost in intuitive leaps that fill the emptiness—the spaces between love and loss— complete. Still we hunger for satiety in a new world where hunger is shared by fullness.... And emptyness is still without form . . . .

And so IT created a human by filling IT (the emptyness) with that which was already there and waiting to be found— knowing that we already knew and still needing to find again and perhaps again and again—a circle of longing and curiosity of satiety and emptiness, hunger and contentment.The ouroboros, The snake biting its tail . . . lacking only flesh and intention. . . .

The human soul swimming in emptiness, tumbling in the ether filled itself with intuition and cellular knowledge—for a great long time—the bones and flesh—buoyant fluids tumbling in a matterless cosmos from nothingness that did and did not long for solidity or definition . . . and so on and on . . .

After—**the creator**—over the matter of a scarce billion years encouraged the matryx which was forming by the random spinning and tangling of matterless matter—revolve or spin or swim in the air that was also the sea—together or side by side , a hodgepodge— roughly, randomly, tentatively in sequences transparent—moved by an ever increasing light—by the way—of intuition and imagination and magic—by the loving of ITself—as yet and still without true substance or attachment . . . Overwhelmed by instability at best. Randomly and seemingly inconsequential—

First up IT recognized reflection—a tentative concept (of time and numbers ?) (A mirror?) and looking into it (created ITS own image) (imagining the I while still falling weightlessly through the emptiness) testing the concept of permanent matter still free and mutable—while tumbling weightless in an empty universe. In time and insistence on something—on making a thing that had no substance but neverthe less surrounded the empty space and was its imagined guard and gardener

Of the opposition eschewing the cushion of agreement that exists only because there is no opposite—*purpose* . . . *finally ultimately IT courted* disagreement and causality— causality and dissuasion

this idea of wo/man may have been the first idea—the inception= of a god of God, All these intentions unintentionally spinning and tumbling, exploding and randomly regrouping— and sticking where they stuck a pattern that recreated itself in new choices repatterning older choices . . . through billions of years of freely floating experimentation . . . .

Still ONE is forced to hold ONE's breath and imagine—a single thought—a unification of opposites which is still billions of years in the future in an imagining that has not to date had a fixed intention—the will and the space and time to be imagined.., to fill a designated space and timeless/time . . .

Until it imagined it had all that IT needed—with the tail in its mouth—and so it was and so it was so. . . . EIN SOF (without end)

Provincetown, 2023/2024

It Looks Like a Life
Memento Mori

I'm sure from the outside
It looks like a life
Even a good life
A productive life
An interesting life
Especially for my age . . .

From the inside
It sometimes feels like a sham
Like a pretend life
Like a child's life
A child still knocking on the door
Its fists are sore

Hawking died last week
The body that housed his brain
stopped pulsing
I suppose I thought he would live forever
Since he already had
The radiant energy
That lifted him softly

Going gently
From that good life
Proving brains are sexy

> *Provincetown, MA*
> *March 14, 2018*

109

Dark Thoughts—and Remembered Dreamings

He was standing by the stairway
as I descended—
lowering my left leg with the bad knee
without bending it
And then my right knee—also carefully

I saw his profile first
and it did an odd thing to my stomach
which was now hiding somewhere
at the back of my throat

I am falling forward
deafened by an avalanche
of annotated possibilities

tumbling down the side of the mountain
boulders to the left of me—jibbers to the right
There is no time for prevarication

then it is still again
A bird is warbling
as before—
And a breeze leads the trees
In a chorus of sweet lament
Heaven sent

the sun blinking through
a stand of Japanese willow
and a late summer sunflower
peeking through the slatted gate

It's getting late
Stripes of early evening
Escape through the fencing
And line up for the count

A chorus of crickets carry on
A distant buzz saw scrapes the air
Ebony castanets a recalcitrant leaky faucet
And the diminished cries of what might be
A coyote or just a lonely dog in the fog

I can see the man with the profile
He turns to face me
His mouth shaped in a remembered scream
Der Schrei der Nature

Don't be fooled
By all this foolishness—
The smoke of abrogated reason
Shooting ducks is out of season
He contends doffing his hat

But he is not the one
He has a sympathetic face
And soulful eyes
But he is not the one—*numero uno*
I must climb back up the mountain

Provincetown, 2019

The author

Artist, activist, actor, dancer, director, expressive arts therapist, horticulturist, gallerist, painter, poet, printmaker, professor, teacher, and Zen practitioner, Bunny Pearlman has lived a vivid, adventuresome life.

From her 1940s post-war childhood in Queens, NY, her love of the winding road drew her to the deserts of Israel, canals of Venice, redwoods of Northern California, beaches of Florida, mountains of Colorado, prairies of South Dakota and arts communities of Mexico, New York, New Jersey and New England.

For many years, Provincetown, MA, was her home base for her peripatetic inquiry into the healing power and the joy which is connected with storytelling. Now, as she is nearing 90, it is her year-round home with cat Gilligan, her garden and a wealth of stories to share.

"Self-portrait as Fellini Babe"
Bunny Pearlman 2019, Provincetown, MA
gouache and pencil on clayboard 8" x 10"